American Moments

ABDO
&
Daughters

THE PILGRIMS

Rachel A. Koestler-Grack

VISIT US AT
WWW.ABDOPUB.COM

Published by ABDO Publishing Company, 4940 Viking Drive, Suite 622, Edina, Minnesota 55435. Copyright © 2005 by Abdo Consulting Group, Inc. International copyrights reserved in all countries. No part of this book may be reproduced in any form without written permission from the publisher. ABDO & Daughters™ is a trademark and logo of ABDO Publishing Company.

Printed in the United States.

Edited by: Melanie A. Howard
Interior Production and Design: Terry Dunham Incorporated
Cover Design: Mighty Media
Photos: Corbis, North Wind Pictures

Library of Congress Cataloging-in-Publication Data

Koestler-Grack, Rachel A., 1973-
    The pilgrims / Rachel A. Koestler-Grack.
        p. cm. -- (American moments)
    Includes index.
    ISBN 1-59197-937-4
    1. Pilgrims (New Plymouth Colony)--Juvenile literature. 2.
Massachusetts--History--New Plymouth, 1620-1691--Juvenile literature. I. Title. II.
Series.

F68.K64 2005
974.4'02--dc22

                                                              2004066001

CONTENTS

LAND HO!

In the middle of the Atlantic Ocean, the *Mayflower* was caught in a violent storm. Suddenly, a sail beam cracked in the gales. Crew members worried the beam would break, putting the ship in peril. Captain Christopher Jones, however, refused to turn back. He ordered the beam braced and the *Mayflower* continued on course for North America.

The *Mayflower*'s courageous passengers would later become known as the Pilgrims. The Pilgrims began their trip from Plymouth, England, in September 1620. They had been at sea for many weeks, cramped and seasick. Every passenger longed for a glimpse of land.

The Pilgrims hadn't known what to expect on their journey. They were unaccustomed to sea travel. A year earlier, 180 colonists had sailed to Jamestown in present-day Virginia. One hundred and thirty of the passengers had died at sea. The Pilgrims knew the tragic story of these colonists. But they were still determined to go to America, where they could freely practice their religion.

In November, the ship pushed toward the shores of a place called Cape Cod. A voice cried, "Land Ho!" The Pilgrims went down on their knees and thanked God. Captain Jones knew the land they had spotted was Cape Cod. The Pilgrims had permission to settle land included in the Virginia Company grant. This land extended north

The Mayflower

The Pilgrims kneel during a prayer meeting on the Mayflower's *deck.*

only to 41 degrees latitude. The land surrounding Cape Cod was north of this line. Captain Jones called a conference on deck. He asked the Pilgrims if they wanted to take land here or continue south.

The Pilgrims wanted to have full legal rights to their plantation, or colony. Above the 41 degree line, their permission patent was useless. Captain Jones and the colonists decided to sail southwest to the mouth of the Hudson River. This area was within the Virginia Company territory. The captain planned to sail around the tip of the Cape and head toward present-day New York. However, the ship ran into sandbars along the coast. Captain Jones had no choice but to turn back to the Cape.

The following day, they sailed into Provincetown Harbor. The Pilgrims decided it was God's will for them to settle at Plymouth, though it was north of the boundaries of their patent.

The Pilgrims land at Plymouth in present-day Massachusetts.

On December 11, 1620, a group of Pilgrims made their first landing at Plymouth. An exploring party found the land there had already been cleared and was ready for settlement. The area was once a village of the Pawtuxet Native Americans. Within the last five years, English explorers had visited the area. They brought European diseases. The Pawtuxet had no resistance to these diseases. They died, and their village disappeared. English captain John Smith had already named the place New Plymouth after an English town.

Unfortunately, winter had already taken hold of the New England countryside. The Pilgrims would have to wait until spring to settle on land. They had to spend the cold winter aboard the *Mayflower*. The terrible journey across the ocean had passed. But new hardships were soon to visit the unsuspecting colonists, who had already endured many difficulties for their religion.

SEARCHING FOR RELIGOUS FREEDOM

By the mid-1500s, England was caught up in a religious revolution known as the Reformation. This religious movement began in the early part of the century. It resulted in widespread rebellion against the Roman Catholic Church.

Catholicism had been the major religion in western Europe for centuries. However, internal corruption and the church's increasing involvement in political affairs caused a great deal of tension. People such as Martin Luther and John Calvin began advocating religious reform.

Then in 1527, King Henry VIII of England sought a divorce from his wife, Catherine of Aragon. He and Catherine had not managed to have a male heir to succeed Henry VIII to the throne.

Anne Boleyn

8

Henry VIII

This concerned the king. Henry VIII had also taken an interest in one of the ladies in his court, Anne Boleyn. He wanted to marry her instead.

Pope Clement VII, however, refused to allow a divorce until he'd had time to review the case. Henry VIII became angry that the pope would not grant him a divorce. In 1532, he split from the Roman Catholic Church. He formed the Anglican Church, and fixed himself as the head of the church.

A group of people soon formed within the Anglican Church who wanted to purify it of Roman Catholic influences. Most of this group of purifiers, or Puritans, wanted to reform the existing church, not create a new one. However, some Puritans thought the Church was too corrupt to be fixed. They separated from the Church of England altogether and formed their own churches. They became known as Separatists. One such church was in Scrooby, England.

At this time, a law stated that all Englishmen must belong to and support the Anglican Church. Being a member of a separatist church was a serious crime. Dissenters were brutally persecuted or punished for disobeying the law. Some separatist leaders were even executed for their beliefs. By the beginning of the 1600s, both separatists and Puritans were increasingly harassed by the English government.

Scrooby members decided they were unsafe in England. They chose to leave their homes behind and flee to Holland, where citizens could worship as they chose. In 1607, the Pilgrims made their first attempt to leave England. They hired a ship to take them to Holland. But the ship's captain betrayed them to the English government. Officers of the king arrested the Pilgrims and charged them with trying to leave the country illegally. They were thrown into jail. After 30 days, all but seven prisoners had been released and sent home.

In the spring of 1608, the Pilgrims tried again. This time, they chose to rendezvous with a Dutch ship off a deserted area of the coast. On the day they were to set sail, the men came to the meeting place by land. But the women and children met the vessel in a small sailing boat called a bark. Strong winds tossed the little bark to and fro. The passengers were unable to climb aboard the larger ship.

Westminster Abbey is one of the most famous Anglican institutions in England. The oldest parts of the abbey were founded as a Roman Catholic monastery by Edward the Confessor in 1065 AD.

A brick from the Pilgrims' church in Leyden, Holland

Wet and seasick, the women convinced the captain to wait until the weather calmed down. While they were waiting, the tide fell, causing the bark to become grounded. The Pilgrims had to wait for high tide the next day before they could set sail.

The Dutch ship sent a smaller boat to get the men as they waited for the bark. As the first boatload of them reached the ship, armed men appeared in the distance. The Dutch captain raised his sails and left the coast, with the men still aboard. The women and children were stranded.

After two failed attempts, the Pilgrims finally made it to Holland. They chose to live in Holland because people could worship freely there. At this time, no other place in western Europe offered religious freedom. The Pilgrims established a church in Leyden and lived there from 1609 to 1620.

For the most part, the Pilgrims enjoyed their time in Leyden. They managed to build homes and find work. Yet, even though their lives were thriving, the Pilgrims were still exiles. They lived in a country where people spoke a different language and had a different heritage.

The Pilgrims valued their English heritage. If they stayed in Holland, their children would either be aliens of the country or become Dutchmen. Neither of these options appealed to the Pilgrims. By 1617, some of the Pilgrims suggested moving to the American colonies.

Other members opposed the dangerous move. In the end, the Pilgrims decided that all great actions are accompanied by great difficulties. They believed they possessed the courage to overcome these challenges. The final decision was made. They would sail for the New World.

The Pilgrims left Holland in the Speedwell.

TO AMERICA!

The Pilgrims now had to decide where to settle and how they would raise money for the trip. The first task was easy. They would choose a place in the area owned by the Virginia Company. In 1606, King James I granted a charter to two trading companies. These companies controlled titles to land on the east coast of North America. The territory stretched between 34 degrees and 45 degrees north latitude. This area extended from present-day North Carolina to Maine.

The Virginia Company owned the rights to settle land up to 41 degrees. The Pilgrims knew the company had already established a successful settlement at Jamestown. With this decided, the Pilgrims sent two agents to London, England, in 1617. These men would try to get the patent, or right to settle, from the Virginia Company.

In London, the agents met a businessman named Thomas Weston. Weston offered to help the Pilgrims get a patent from the Virginia Company. But his help would not come free. Weston was interested in making a profit. He would invest money in the colonists by purchasing their passage to the New World. The Pilgrims originally agreed to work with Weston as a joint-stock company for seven years. During these years, all profits made by the colonists would be shared with Weston's company.

James I

But Weston later demanded that all personal property, such as houses and gardens, also be shared. The Pilgrims thought these things should belong to the planter from the beginning. Also, the colonists wanted two days of the week to work for themselves. Weston required every day to be shared profit. The agents accepted Weston's terms without consulting the Pilgrims. Back in Holland, the Pilgrims became angry when they learned of the new terms. The agents argued that if they wanted to go to America, they must agree to Weston's terms.

On July 22, 1620, a group of Pilgrims boarded the ship *Speedwell*. Passengers said good-bye to family and friends. On August 5, the *Speedwell* arrived at Southhampton, England. There, the Pilgrims first saw the mighty cargo ship *Mayflower*.

The *Mayflower* was stocked with supplies and ready to carry the colonists to America. But the terms with Weston were still unresolved. The Pilgrims insisted they were not bound to the new terms. In turn, Weston stopped all payments for the journey.

To stay on schedule, the Pilgrims were forced to find new funds. With little choice, they sold some provisions. On August 15, 1620, about 120 passengers set sail from Southhampton. After three days at sea, the *Speedwell* began leaking. The *Speedwell*'s captain, William Reynolds, refused to continue. Both ships returned to England and docked at Dartmouth on August 23.

The *Speedwell* was repaired, and the vessels set sail again on August 31. But 300 nautical miles (556 km) later, the *Speewell* again began taking water. Both captains turned their ships around and returned, this time to Plymouth, England.

Marine archaeologists believe the Mayflower was a square-rigged sailing ship that measured 90 feet (27 m) long and weighed 180 tons (163 t).

Pilgrims in this picture sign the Mayflower Compact on the *Mayflower*. The Pilgrims modeled the Mayflower Compact after the covenant of their church. The covenant granted religious authority to Pilgrim church members. An official charter was later granted to the Pilgrims allowing them to settle where they had. However, the Mayflower Compact remained in effect until Plymouth became part of the Massachusetts Bay Colony in 1691. Many sources indicate what the original text of the document was. However, the original compact has either disappeared or was destroyed.

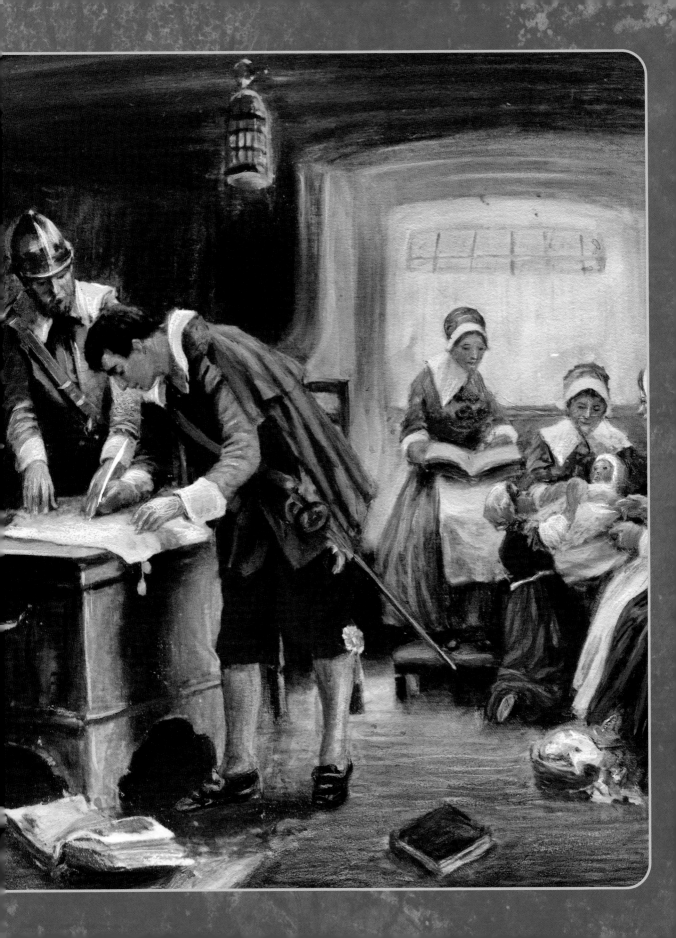

The departure had now been delayed nearly a month. The colonists needed to settle in North America before winter. Any more troubles, and they risked arriving in the New World too late. Instead of chancing another trip with the *Speedwell*, they sold the ship and combined passengers and provisions. Some passengers willingly dropped out and now only 102 Pilgrims remained. On September 6, 1620, the *Mayflower* set sail alone.

Two months at sea wore on the Pilgrims. The constant rocking of the boat caused many passengers to suffer seasickness. When land was spotted on November 19, the colonists were relieved.

On November 21, the *Mayflower* anchored off Provincetown Harbor. Some passengers grew restless and wanted to be independent of the Pilgrims. Since the Pilgrims were settling outside of their patent, they were not bound by English law.

In an effort to keep order, the Pilgrims decided to create a government for the colony. They elected governors and set up laws. Forty-one men signed what later became known as the Mayflower Compact. This historic document was the first foundation of government in the Plymouth settlement. The signatures included all free adult male passengers. John Carver was elected the first governor of Plymouth.

The Pilgrims had crossed the ocean with incredible endurance. They did not yet even have assurance of financial support. But their faith in God and themselves gave them the strength to continue. Their perseverance was sure to be tested in the months ahead.

JAMESTOWN

The first English settlement in the area that would become the United States was Jamestown in present-day Virginia. The colony was named after King James I. It was founded on May 14, 1607. The first representative government and the first Anglican church in the American colonies were established in Jamestown. Also, the first Africans used for labor in the colonies were brought to Jamestown in 1619.

Jamestown declined and nearly disappeared after the colony's capital was moved to Williamsburg in 1699. After several preservation efforts and archaeological digs, some parts of the original buildings have been uncovered. The only building left standing at the site is the church tower. Nevertheless, it was made a national historic park in 1934.

The Susan Constant, the Godspeed, and the Discovery brought the first settlers to Jamestown.

SURVIVING A HARSH WINTER

With winter fast approaching, the possibility of building a permanent settlement looked grim. From the *Mayflower*, North America looked like a desolate wilderness. The Pilgrims knew the nearest English settlement was hundreds of miles away. They had no homes to live in and no fort to defend them from possible native attacks. After being confined to the ship for 11 weeks, the colonists were weak. They had tried to make do with a poor diet and damp clothing. But by mid-November, many passengers were sick.

For more than a month, the *Mayflower* anchored in Cape Cod. During the first few days, men went ashore and chopped firewood. The women washed clothes. The Pilgrims began searching for a suitable place to build a settlement.

As they explored the territory, they discovered storage pits filled with corn. These supplies belonged to the Wampanoag Native Americans. But the colonists believed God had led them to find the corn. They would now have seeds to plant in the spring. They took the supplies for themselves. The Wampanoag thought the Pilgrims were thieves.

The Pilgrims decided they could not build a plantation in Cape Cod. On Saturday, December 7, a group of men took a small boat called a shallop to explore other options. The men thought the

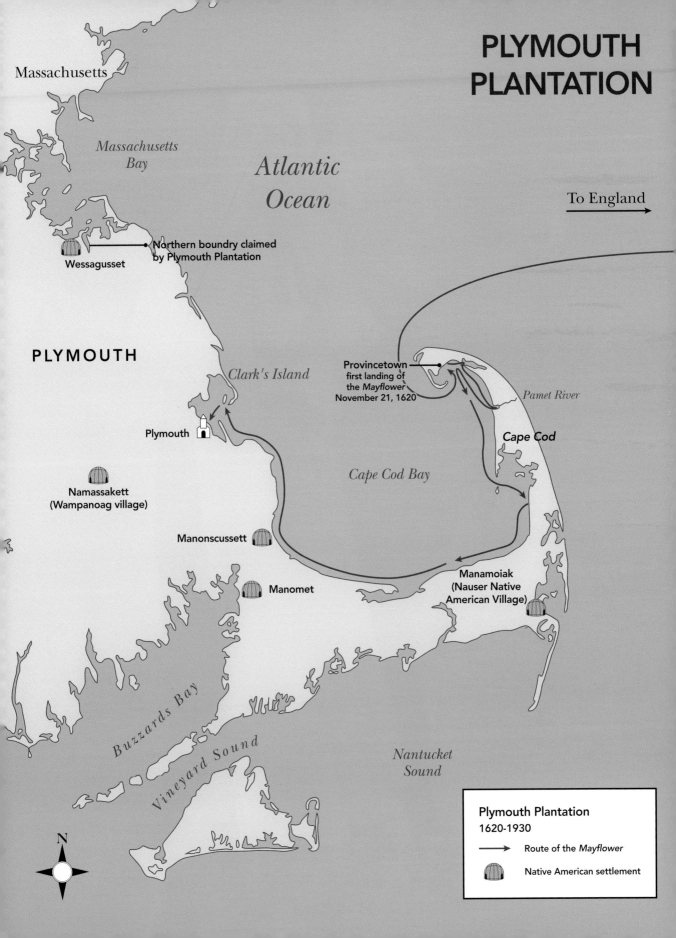

PLYMOUTH
PLANTATION

Massachusetts

Massachusetts Bay

Atlantic Ocean

To England

Northern boundry claimed by Plymouth Plantation

Wessagusset

PLYMOUTH

Clark's Island

Provincetown
first landing of
the *Mayflower*
November 21, 1620

Pamet River

Plymouth

Cape Cod

Namassakett
(Wampanoag village)

Cape Cod Bay

Manonscussett

Manomet

Manamoiak
(Nauser Native
American Village)

Buzzards Bay

Nantucket Sound

Vineyard Sound

N

| Plymouth Plantation |
| 1620-1930 |
| → Route of the *Mayflower* |
| Native American settlement |

A Pilgrim couple

Plymouth Bay area would be suitable for settlement. They returned to the *Mayflower*, excited to share their discovery.

Unfortunately, by the time the *Mayflower* arrived in Plymouth Bay on December 16, four people had died. These included future governor William Bradford's wife, Dorothy. For the next week, an exploring party searched for a plantation site. Inland, they found an abandoned Native American village. They believed this would be an ideal place for a colony.

The English colonists believed the land was free to take. To them, the Native Americans were too uncivilized to use the land properly. One colonist wrote, "Their land is spacious and void. . . .They are not industrious, neither have art, science, skill or faculty to use either the land or the commodities of it . . . so it is lawful now to take a land which none useth."

But the Native Americans had used the land for thousands of years. The English people simply did not understand the natives' way of life. All they saw was that it did not look like Europe. The Pilgrims began building homes at Plymouth on December 25.

The winter proved to be harsh. Most of the Pilgrims continued to live on the ship throughout the winter months. Chilled by the damp, cold air, many Pilgrims fell ill. Those who stayed well took care of their sick friends. When the weather was nice, they worked at the plantation.

However, trouble continued for the settlers. In January, a fire destroyed the thatched roof of the storehouse. Some of the Pilgrims' precious supplies were lost in the fire. The Pilgrims tried hard not to loose faith. But sadness seemed to visit them day after day as sick people died. Before spring, nearly half of the Pilgrims were dead.

THANKSGIVING

On March 16, 1621, the Pilgrims received a visit from Samoset, a leader of the Abenaki people. This Native American tribe lived to the north of Plymouth. Samoset surprised the settlers because he could speak English. He was there to gather information for Wampanoag leader Massasoit. Samoset hoped to find out if the English people wanted peace or war.

Massasoit himself later met with Plymouth governor John Carver. The two leaders made formal rules about how the two peoples would act toward each other. Both sides needed a peaceful alliance. The Wampanoag people had lost many members to disease. They also knew the English had powerful weapons. The Pilgrims had guns and gunpowder. But they were still few in number compared to the natives. If they joined together, the two groups could protect each other from neighboring tribes.

Accompanying Massasoit was Tisquantum, better known as Squanto. Squanto was a member of

Pilgrims holding muskets

Massasoit meets with Governor John Carver.

the Pawtuxet tribe, which once lived at Plymouth. When Squanto was younger, an English captain kidnapped him and took him to England. He was there for nine years. During this time, he learned to speak English.

In 1614, Squanto was taken to North America as an interpreter with Captain John Smith. He was later taken to Spain and sold as a slave. Somehow, Squanto managed to escape and fled to Holland. Finally in 1619, he made it back to Cape Cod. When he returned home, Squanto learned that disease had killed most of his village. He joined Massasoit's tribe.

Squanto stayed with the Pilgrims after Massasoit left. He showed them the best places to fish. He also taught them to plant corn using fish as fertilizer. Squanto served as a translator between the Pilgrims and other Native American groups.

Pilgrims build the Plymouth colony.

The First Thanksgiving *by Jennie Augusta Brownscombe*

The Pilgrims worked hard that first summer to build their plantation. They put up seven houses and set up plans for more. With seeds brought from England, they planted gardens of carrots, lettuce, beans, cabbage, squash, and peas. They also had access to dried fruit and nuts.

By harvest time, the Pilgrims had plenty of food. They owed much of this to Squanto. The peas and wheat did poorly the first year. But the corn Squanto helped to plant thrived. In England, people celebrated a bountiful crop. The Pilgrims decided to have a harvest feast.

William Bradford had replaced Carver as governor by this time. He sent out a hunting party to shoot fowl for the meal. Nearby Native Americans heard the gunfire. Massasoit went to the colony to find out what the gunfire was for.

When Massasoit arrived, he saw that the Pilgrims were preparing a feast. Native Americans also celebrated harvest festivals of thanksgiving each year. During these festivals, the natives showed their gratitude toward the Creator for giving them food. Often, they shared the harvest with their neighbors.

A painting of the first Thanksgiving by J.L.M. Ferris

Massasoit sent some of his men out to hunt deer. They brought back five deer to add to the feast. Wampanoag women and children were also invited to join the celebration. For three days, the Pilgrims, Squanto, and the Wampanoag tribe feasted and played games.

Today, no one is certain what the colonists and the Wampanoag ate on that first Thanksgiving in Plymouth. They may have eaten venison, turkey, duck, or partridge. They may also have served lobster, clams, herring, cod, or bass. There were also cornmeal and pumpkin available to them.

When the Pilgrims feasted in 1621, it was not a religious gathering. Most likely, it was a harvest festival, similar to the ones they had celebrated in England. To the pilgrims the word thanksgiving did not mean a festival with feasting. It meant a religious service of worship.

The first religious thanksgiving day in Plymouth happened in 1623. This was two years after the Pilgrims and Wampanoag gathered. However, the colonists continued to have harvest celebrations each fall. Thanksgiving became a national holiday in 1863. President Abraham Lincoln declared the last Thursday in November to be a day of thanksgiving for blessings.

Abraham Lincoln

In November 1621, another ship, the *Fortune*, arrived at Plymouth. The ship carried 36 new settlers. More importantly, the colonists brought with them a new patent, making Plymouth a legal settlement. When Captain Jones returned to England, he told Weston the Pilgrims had settled north of the Virginia grant. Weston immediately went to work getting a new patent for his colony.

But the patent also brought new troubles for the colonists. With it, Weston insisted the Pilgrims abide by the terms he had laid out. The Pilgrims had to agree to Weston's terms to gain legal rights to their plantation.

This agreement meant they would have to pay Weston's company half of all their profits. They also needed to find a way to buy more supplies. With Squanto's help, the Pilgrims traded with the Massachuset Native Americans for beaver furs. The colonists sent the valuable furs and some lumber back to England on the *Fortune*.

Unfortunately, the *Fortune* ran into some bad luck. It was captured by the French in the North Atlantic. The valuable cargo was stolen. Without payment, Weston's company refused to send more supplies. Back in Plymouth, the Pilgrims were unaware of *Fortune*'s fate. To their disappointment, the next ship arrived in 1622 without the much needed supplies. Instead, it brought more colonists.

Although more settlers added strength to the plantation, they also placed a heavy burden on Plymouth. Now the plantation needed to find ways to feed and shelter the new colonists. Governor Bradford took a count of all the provisions. Even if each family lived on half rations, the food would only last six months. The Pilgrims would need to get food from the Native Americans.

A woman spins wool into yarn on a spinning wheel. Pilgrims had to make their own clothes when supplies did not arrive.

A GROWING PLYMOUTH

Until 1622, the Pilgrims had kept a good relationship with their Native American neighbors. However, their friend and helper Squanto caused some diplomatic trouble with neighboring tribes, including the Narraganset.

The Narraganset to the west of Plymouth was a powerful tribe. It controlled most of present-day Rhode Island. This Native American group was an enemy of the Massachuset and Wampanoag tribes. In early 1622, Governor Bradford captured a Narraganset runner who carried a message for Squanto. The messenger brought a bundle of arrows tied together with snakeskin.

Squanto said Narraganset chief Canonicus was challenging the Pilgrims. This news troubled Bradford. The Narraganset had more than 5,000 warriors compared to Plymouth's 50 fighting men. Bradford decided that Plymouth must be protected. For six weeks, workers built a palisade around the town. Guards took turns standing watch at the gate.

A Wampanoag named Hobomok was friends with the Pilgrims. He came to Plymouth with important news. Hobomok had heard that the Massachuset tribe had joined the Narraganset and were planning to attack the settlement. Surprisingly, Hobomok said Squanto was involved with the planned attack. The Pilgrims could hardly believe Squanto would betray them.

Squanto visits a Pilgrim home.

After much thought, Bradford decided the Pilgrims were too weak to simply wait to be attacked. The Pilgrims would trade with the Massachuset tribe and find out if the rumor was true. Captain Miles Standish, Squanto, Hobomok, and ten other colonists set out in the shallop.

They had barely pushed off shore when a friend of Squanto's came running down the beach. He claimed the Wampanoag had also joined the Narraganset, and warriors were on their way to Plymouth. He begged the men to go home. Standish couldn't take any chances. He returned to Plymouth and prepared for battle.

Hobomok could not believe that Massasoit would join his enemies against the Pilgrims. He sent his wife to Massasoit's village. There, she found the villagers peacefully going about their daily chores. Hobomok's wife told Massasoit about the panic and rumors in Plymouth. Massasoit immediately sent her back with a message for Bradford. The Wampanoag were still at peace with Plymouth.

Unbelievably, it was Squanto who had started the rumors. Squanto had begun to use his power with the Pilgrims for his own gain. He threatened other natives into giving him gifts. He claimed Plymouth had storage pits filled with the plague. Squanto made other natives believe that if they did not obey him, the Pilgrims would release the disease.

When Massasoit learned that Squanto was misusing his position, he became furious. He insisted the Pilgrims hand Squanto over to him to be executed. According to the peace agreement, Squanto should be given to Massosoit for punishment. Governor Bradford stalled, hoping Massasoit would forgive Squanto. Squanto had done

Miles Standish

so much to help the Pilgrims. Bradford did not want to see Squanto killed. But the governor did not want to damage his relationship with the Wampanoag either.

While Bradford waited for Massasoit's anger to calm, more trouble arose. In June 1622, a ship brought 60 of Weston's men to Plymouth. These men were rude and coarse. They brought no supplies for the town, but demanded to be fed. In the fall, Weston's men left to form a settlement at Wessagasset. Weston's men treated the Native Americans in their area poorly and made many enemies.

The Pilgrims' fall harvest was not good. They would certainly need more food to make it through the winter. In November 1622, the Pilgrims and Weston's men attempted to trade with the Native Americans for food. On this expedition, Squanto fell ill with a fever and died. The colonists were left without an interpreter. They reluctantly decided to return to Plymouth to try to trade with local natives.

By this time, Weston's men had strained relations between the settlers and the Massachuset tribe. The Massachuset refused to trade with the Pilgrims because of the Wessagasset settlement. Without the much needed corn, the winter of 1623 would surely bring famine to Plymouth. Luckily, the colonists found other Native Americans to trade enough corn and beans to survive.

Life at Plymouth changed quickly, and the Pilgrims soon forgot their promises to the Native Americans. In 1630, the population of Plymouth was only about 300. Ten years later, the number of settlers had climbed to almost 2,000. The English needed more land to support the growing colony. Tension grew between the Pilgrims and the Native Americans as the Pilgrims took over more land.

Metacom

In 1675, Massosoit's son, Metacom, rallied many Native American tribes against the Englishmen. Metacom, known to the colonists as Philip, wanted to drive the settlers out of his homeland. He started what became known as King Philip's War.

The war brought terrible consequences to both sides. Many English settlers and Wampanoag died in the battles. Native Americans burned English villages. Colonists captured natives and sold them as slaves to merchants from the West Indies. The war came to a bitter end in 1676. In the end, Metacom was dead and the Wampanoag had lost their independence and much of their homeland.

Few Plymouth settlers seemed to remember the peaceful feast they shared with the Wampanoag 50 years earlier. Instead, the colonists held a new day of thanksgiving. This time, they celebrated the English victory over their native neighbors.

Plymouth became part of the Massachusetts Bay Colony in 1691. It was not until many years later that the Pilgrims would earn credit as founders of New England. The Pilgrims' strength and courage helped build a nation based on freedom. But their victory came at the price of another's freedom, the Native Americans. Hopefully, future generations can use this knowledge to rebuild peace between cultures and once again learn to share a great land.

A replica of a Pilgrim's home at Plimoth Plantation

PLIMOTH PLANTATION

Plimoth Plantation, located in Plymouth, Massachusetts, preserves the history of the Pilgrims. The site includes the Pilgrim Village, a Wampanoag dwelling, and the Mayflower II. In the village, actors portray Pilgrims for visitors. Native Americans at the Wampanoag home site talk to visitors about their history and culture.

TIMELINE

1532   The Reformation occurs in England.

1532   Henry VIII splits from the Roman Catholic Church. He makes himself the head of the new Anglican Church.

1609 to 1620   The Pilgrims emigrate from England to Holland and live and worship in Leyden.

1619   One hundred and eighty colonists sail from England to Jamestown in North America. One hundred and thirty die.

1620   On September 6, the Pilgrims depart from Plymouth, England, for North America.

In November, the *Mayflower* arrives at Cape Cod.

On November 21, 41 Pilgrim men sign the Mayflower Compact.

On December 11, a group of Pilgrims first lands at Plymouth. The Pilgrims soon decide to build their settlement there.

1621 On March 16, Samoset visits the Pilgrims, paving the way for relations with the Wampanoag Native Americans. Wampanoag leader Massasoit soon follows with Squanto.

In the fall, the Pilgrims, the Wampanoag, and Squanto hold a three-day feast to celebrate the harvest. This event comes to be known as the first Thanksgiving.

1622 A group of colonists form another settlement at Wessagasset. They make many enemies among local Native Americans.

1675 to 1676 King Philip's War is fought between the English settlers and allied Native American tribes led by Metacom. The Native Americans lose the war.

1691 Plymouth becomes part of the Massachusetts Bay Colony.

1863 President Abraham Lincoln makes Thanksgiving a national holiday.

American Moments

FAST FACTS

The word *Wampanoag* means People of the Light. They are also known as People of the First Light and People of the East. The Wampanoag traditionally refer to themselves simply as the People.

Many illustrations of Pilgrims show the colonists wearing dark clothes and large hats with silver buckles. In truth, Pilgrims dressed very colorfully, in red, green, blue, or purple.

In 1863, President Abraham Lincoln actually declared two national Thanksgivings. The other Thanksgiving was held in August to honor the Civil War's Battle of Gettysburg. At least 10,000 people were killed or fatally wounded in this battle.

Today, many Wampanoag people meet at the statue of Massasoit in Plymouth, Massachusetts, on Thanksgiving Day. For them, it is a day of mourning. They use this time to remember the struggles of their ancestors.

The *Mayflower II* at Plimoth Plantation was created between 1955 and 1957 in Devon, England. Warwick Charlton decided to make the ship to show how ties between the United States and England had been strengthened during World War II. The *Mayflower II* is much like the original *Mayflower*. However, the ship has a modern staircase and electric lighting to aid tourists who come to view it.

WEB SITES
WWW.ABDOPUB.COM

Would you like to learn more about the Pilgrims? Please visit **www.abdopub.com** to find up-to-date Web site links about the Pilgrims and other American moments. These links are routinely monitored and updated to provide the most current information available.

Legend states that the Pilgrims first stepped onshore at Plymouth Rock. The rock has been preserved. But there is little evidence to support the story that the Pilgrims first set foot here.

GLOSSARY

Anglican Church: a Protestant church that arose in England in the sixteenth century. The Anglican Church is also called the Church of England.

commodity: advantage or benefit.

dissenter: one who refuses to accept the established church.

faculty: ability.

heritage: something handed down from one generation to the next.

joint-stock company: a company made up of people who pool their fortunes together. In the 1600s, investors formed a joint-stock company called the Virginia Company to gain profit from colonizing the New World.

palisade: a fence of strong stakes placed closely together and set firmly

    into the ground.

perseverance: persistent determination.

ration: a fixed amount of food that has to last an exact amount of time.

rendezvous: to meet.

Roman Catholic Church: one of the main branches of Christianity. The

    Roman Catholic Church is headed by the pope.

separatists: people who want to be governed separately and independently.

thatch: straw, reeds, or similar material used to cover a roof.

INDEX